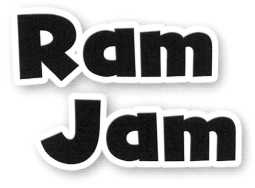

Ram Jam

by Pearl Markovics

Consultant:
Beth Gambro
Reading Specialist
Yorkville, Illinois

Contents

BEARPORT
PUBLISHING

New York, New York

Ram Jam

Let's rhyme!

This is **Pam**.

Pam was hungry.
So she ate some **ham**.

Later, **Pam swam.**

Then, **Pam** visited her pet **ram**.

His name is
Sam the **ram**.

Sam really loves **jam.**

Pam says, "Scram!"

Jam is not good for **Sam**.

Key Words in the -am Family

ham

jam

ram

scram

swam

Other **-am** Words:
dam, exam, scam, yam

Index

About the Author

Pearl Markovics enjoys having fun with words. She especially likes witty wordplay.

Teaching Tips

Before Reading

✔ Introduce rhyming words and the **-am** word family to readers.

✔ Guide readers on a "picture walk" through the text by asking them to name the things shown.

✔ Discuss book structure by showing children where text will appear consistently on pages. Highlight the supportive pattern of the book.

During Reading

✔ Encourage readers to "read with your finger" and point to each word as it is read. Stop periodically to ask children to point to a specific word in the text.

✔ Reading strategies: When encountering unknown words, prompt readers with encouraging cues such as:

  • **Does that word look like a word you already know?**
  • **Does it rhyme with another word you have already read?**

After Reading

✔ Write the key words on index cards.

  • **Have readers match them to pictures in the book.**

✔ Ask readers to identify their favorite page in the book. Have them read that page aloud.

✔ Choose an **-am** word. Ask children to pick a word that rhymes with it.

✔ Ask children to create their own rhymes using **-am** words. Encourage them to use the same pattern found in the book.

Credits: Cover, Eric Isselee/Shutterstock and © Nils Z/Shutterstock; 2–3, © Africa Studio/Shutterstock and © PavelShynkarou/Shutterstock; 4–5, © P Maxwell Photography/Shutterstock, © Africa Studio/Shutterstock, and © weedezign/Shutterstock; 6–7, © LightField Studios/Shutterstock; 8–9, © Africa Studio/Shutterstock, © Eric Isselee/Shutterstock, and © Artazum/Shutterstock; 10–11, © Eric Isselee/Shutterstock, © Igor Sokolov/Shutterstock, and © bogdan ionescu/Shutterstock; 12–13, © Eric Isselee/Shutterstock, © N-sky/Shutterstock, © Nils Z/Shutterstock, and © donatas1205/Shutterstock; 14, © Africa Studio/Shutterstock and © Nils Z/Shutterstock; 15, © Cookedphotos/iStock and © Eric Isselee/Shutterstock; 16T (L to R), © P Maxwell Photography/Shutterstock, © Nils Z/Shutterstock, and © Eric Isselee/Shutterstock; 16B (L to R), © Cookedphotos/iStock and © LightField Studios/Shutterstock.

Publisher: Kenn Goin   **Senior Editor**: Joyce Tavolacci   **Creative Director**: Spencer Brinker

Library of Congress Cataloging-in-Publication Data: Names: Markovics, Pearl, author. | Gambro, Beth, consultant. Title: Ram jam / by Pearl Markovics; consultant: Beth Gambro, Reading Specialist. Description: New York, New York: Bearport Publishing, [2020] | Series: Read and rhyme: level 2 | Includes index. Identifiers: LCCN 2019007618 (print) | LCCN 2019010564 (ebook) | ISBN 9781642806052 (ebook) | ISBN 9781642805512 (library) | ISBN 9781642807134 (pbk.) Subjects: LCSH: Readers (Primary) Classification: LCC PE1119 (ebook) | LCC PE1119 .M2858 2 0202 (print) | DDC 428.6/2–dc23 LC record available at https://lccn.loc.gov/2019007618

10 9 8 7 6 5 4 3 2 1